CountryFail

CountryFail

*Some C***'s Guide
to the Countryside*

KILLIAN SUNDERMANN

faber

First published in 2024
by Faber & Faber Ltd
The Bindery, 51 Hatton Garden
London EC1N 8HN

Typeset by Faber & Faber Ltd
Printed in the UK by CPI Group (UK) Ltd, Croydon, CR0 4YY

IMAGES
Dora Kazmierak © pages 1, 7, 19, 55, 81, 105
Shutterstock © pages 11, 23, 30, 31, 35, 38, 41, 45, 51, 53,
60, 62, 67, 71, 87, 95, 103

A CIP record for this book
is available from the British Library

ISBN 978-0-571-38945-2

MIX
Paper | Supporting
responsible forestry
FSC® C171272

Printed and bound in the UK on FSC® certified paper in line with our continuing
commitment to ethical business practices, sustainability and the environment.
For further information see faber.co.uk/environmental-policy

2 4 6 8 10 9 7 5 3 1

Contents

Foreword

Months ago, mildly popular social media star Killian Sundermann, better known by his social media handle @killersundy, deleted all his social media accounts, moved to an undisclosed rural area and, in his own words, 'went native'. In a dramatic and what would turn out to be final Instagram post, he lampooned the online comedy scene, stating it was 'all focused on the numbers and nothing to do with actual artistic endeavour'. This was broadly seen as a reaction to the plummeting numbers and engagements on his recent videos, the large drop-off in his followers across all platforms, and what was generally agreed upon as a severe reduction in the quality of his work.

Bar a few sightings, the young comedian has not been seen in public for several weeks since his farewell post. He is understood to be living in a van in an unspecified location. 'Sayonara, sheeple,' his last post read. 'While you are all slaves to the brain vacuum machine that is social media, I'm going off-grid to live a utopian dream in literal paradise.' An IP address search on that post revealed his location to be the public restrooms in a service station off the M7 motorway.

It wasn't until a few weeks ago that Sundermann re-emerged into public life, having rebranded himself as a 'countryside influencer', and shared the following post.

In my online sketches, I completed the urban assessment: I figured it out and showed it to the world for what it was, a bastardisation of corporate greed, a dishevelment of morality in the common person and an absolute lack of understanding or appreciation for someone who is trying to make avant-garde comedy sketches (see my series about the embarrassing feeling you get when buying toilet paper). The city is done, it is finished. Nobody is interested any more – get over it, London; move on, Hong Kong. Now I will shift my focus to the countryside, the final frontier of life, where flora and fauna rule the roost and the muddy fingernails of the common working farmer achieve more in a morning's back-breaking labour than any 'influencer' would in a thousand sponsored posts. And no, I haven't done any back-breaking labour to figure that out; as an empath, I could tell just by watching.

The same day, he was seen dropping a manuscript, written entirely on what appeared to be McDonald's takeaway bags, at the doors of Faber's offices. The drop-off was not publicised or acknowledged and a few days later Sundermann took to social media to berate the distinguished publishers for trying to silence him and hiding vital information from the public.

These are people who published Joyce and Beckett, they should know a thing or two about transgressive Irish authors, but here they are, silencing me. They have the only copy too, they know exactly what they're doing, and yes maybe I should have duplicated the manuscript, but it was really hard to fit the McDonald's paper bags into a photocopying machine. No matter what shape I cut it, the paper was too thick to fit in. In fact, that's another thing I want to talk about . . .

In the midst of this storm of posts, an intrepid intern from Faber who had been following Sundermann's rant put two and two together and managed to locate the manuscript in the bin outside the department she'd left it in.

Faber took the liberty of transcribing the text and are delighted to present to the public an unedited version, now titled *CountryFail*, with images courtesy of Faber and some from the author himself.

INTRODUCTION
Welcome, city dweller!

Before we go skipping together through green fields, one question must be addressed, to prepare you for the journey ahead: *What is the countryside?* It is often described as 'not town, not city', which frankly leaves a lot to be desired. If that which is not a city is therefore countryside, my cousin Solly must also, by this definition, be the countryside. Can we spend a weekend away in a converted-barn-turned-expensive-Airbnb on my cousin Solly's back? No, of course not. For starters, Solly doesn't do squats, so his back can barely support his own weight, let alone a couple having a romantic trip away together.

To say the countryside is simply not the city is a philosophy of such arrogance that it's quite clear it was written by a city dweller (yes, this is the politically correct term). It was he (yes, 'he' – it was definitely a man, probably working in finance, who came up with it in between his busy schedule of gym/buddha bowl/coffee/work/lunch/coffee/work/gym/Netflix/ being numbed into a fitful, protein-shake-induced sleep) who declared the countryside to be *that which isn't city*. He was probably called Dave. Yes, I'm getting serious Dave vibes from this person.

As a man of two weeks' lived experience of the countryside, I feel best placed to offer up an alternative to Dave's meagre attempt. So, how to describe this place, full of animals, farms and forests, streams and ditches, faerie forts and the occasional fly-tipped mattress? This idyllic space, which has managed to avoid the full brunt of humanity and look all the better for it? Well, I challenge you to better this:

Countryside (noun) – the one place other than Glastonbury you'll need to wear wellies.

A History: Paradise Lost

In the beginning, it was all countryside. Flora and fauna blossomed. Animals ran together in perfect harmony, frolicking naked through the forest. Drifting clouds of bees tickled the flowers, spreading wealth, nature and joy all over Mother Earth's beautiful land.

Dublin, before the Industrial Revolution.

Then, with an unceremonious splat, an unfortunate-looking fish wheezed itself out of the sea it had called home for millions of years and decided it preferred the clean air on land to having to sift water, salt and its own urine through its cheeks in order to breathe. Within a few million years, this fish had become what we know as the modern human and had rearranged Mother Earth's complex natural system to entirely suit its own needs and desires. Forests were chopped down to build homes, pesticides were sprayed so that apples looked redder, and whole species of animals became extinct because they tasted so delicious.

But mankind didn't destroy *all* the magical green spaces of the countryside. It was, after all, a place where they could survey the landscape, take a deep breath and say 'Now isn't this nice?' and declare themselves to 'feel human' again, before leaving their soggy sandwiches and litter behind as they returned to the city. Some people did live there, but they weren't the loud, busy ones; they were the contemplative, friendly ones. And farmers.

In order for us to fully understand the countryside and all that it contains, I will take you now on a journey – or a ramble – and as we stroll together I will orate and impart to you the deep wisdom and understanding of the countryside that I have gained from the many, long last couple of weeks I have lovingly spent here.

I know it might come as a shock to you, but I was not always a man of the countryside. Before I transcended to the higher plane of country strolls and nice fresh air that I currently occupy, I was once like you, a mindless cog in the ever-turning wheel of the city. I was one of the worst, the filthiest rat in the rat race. I crawled to depths of despair nobody had seen before, but it was all part of my journey. I had to reach my lowest, in order to be rebuilt into the oracle of natural wisdom that I have now become.

Modern life is a torment, a state of being in which we have been conditioned from birth to chase profitability and glory within the market, and for what? What's the best that could happen? Sure, you could achieve a mild level of fame. Maybe even get your videos shared in the work WhatsApp. Occasionally, people might recognise you when you're out and about, you might get the occasional thirsty DM, but eventually your fifteen minutes will slip away; people will stop sharing your work, they will stop going to your shows, they will stop appreciating you. Why? Because they are fickle and wouldn't know true art if it danced naked in front of them with the *Mona Lisa* painted on its buttocks. Indeed, they will stop calling you and, soon afterwards, even stop answering your calls. The people who were there for your good times, well, suddenly they will be gone and you will find that the payments for the bloated apartment in the city centre that you got at an extremely volatile, variable mortgage rate, because you thought you'd pay it off in a couple of years, ends up being the anchor tied to your ankle as you suddenly plummet to the watery depths of bankruptcy. Before you know it, you're forced to downsize into a Ford Transit van that was converted by some hippy in Waterford and, to survive, you move to a remote part of Clare, where one of your few remaining loyal fans, a pensioner named Mairead, will let you park on her property and use her electricity in exchange for giving German lessons to her frankly obnoxious child, Eric, who simply cannot grasp the subtle differences between dative and accusative prepositions.

But this experience of being thrown out of society and ignored will turn out to be the blessing in disguise that you were always looking for. Sure, you don't have running water. Sure, you can't fully extend your legs as you sleep and now you have developed a hunched, goblin-like physique. Sure, when nature calls in the middle of the night and you don't feel like facing the cold outdoors you find yourself peeing into a milk carton in a van in rural countryside, but isn't this what life is *really* about, when you think about it? Life strips you away from the twenty-first-century comforts we've surrounded ourselves with. Far away from back-stabbers and hangers-on, your poetry is improving dramatically, despite what Mairead and Eric say, and your head has never felt clearer. One day, an epiphany engulfs your mind, as you realise that you have figured out the solution to anxiety, apathy and loneliness in this late-stage capitalist world. And you realise it is time to share it with everyone else. Maybe you'll get a book deal, maybe you'll get on the telly again, maybe people will once again call to you on the street and kiss your hands in forgiveness for turning their attention elsewhere, even for the briefest of moments. It's not why you're doing it – you are an altruistic person, of course – but you will be king once more and all will bow to your majesty and humility as you magnanimously welcome them back to your bosom. Hypothetically speaking, of course.

So, put on your favourite pair of hiking boots, zip up the breathable windbreaker that you bought for an extortionate amount of money in one of those outdoor shops that you never go into because the red-bearded men in hiking gear intimidate you with their strong legs and their practical spoons that with the right application can also be used as a fishing rod. Pull over your ears the dusty, moth-ravaged woollen hat that hasn't seen the light of day for a whole year and now more resembles (and smells like) a limp, raggedy sock, and meet me in the morning at the small grassy knoll over by the forest. And just as the sun is peeking over the horizon to bring in a new day, together we will ramble, over hill and through dale and stream, under trees and around the bush, through the countryside.

PART I

What a countryside!

To begin our journey through the countryside, I will first show you some of its key features, the veritable building blocks of the land: fields, hedges, stone walls and trees. These are terms that you have perhaps seen in films or heard tell of in ancient tales, but have you ever actually seen any of them in real life? I doubt it, cement-lover.

The steep bits

Identifying the different topography of the countryside is a vitally important step to surviving in the wilds. There are many traps laid by Mother Nature for a naive city dweller to fall into.

First things first: if you spend any amount of time in the countryside, you're going to encounter a hill, which can be incredibly dangerous. So you'll have to know how to identify one. Hills are not to be confused with holes. They *sound* very similar in name but are dangerously different when you encounter them in nature. The golden rule is: hills go up; holes go down. So be very careful, because even I, though a seasoned and respected man of the outdoors (I taught Bear Grylls how to drink his own urine), have many times walked towards what I thought was a hill, only to fall down what turned out to be a hole. The best way to remember it is that the letter 'i' in hill goes up, and the letter 'o' in hole looks like a hole.

As we know, hills are there for walking up, because the top of the hill is the best place to look at things. Mountains are different. They're like hills, but they go up more: they're for *looking* at, not walking up. Some people do walk up them, but that's because they have emotional issues.

The Alps are particularly popular with men
who have just been dumped.

The blank-space bits

To help demonstrate what a hill is, I take you
for a leisurely stroll up one. 'What is that?' I hear
you wheeze, in between gasping breaths from a
few metres behind me (because you are finding
it hard to keep up with my strong, steady, athletic
pace). 'What is what?' I respond in a calm tone,
seemingly unaware of the impressive speed at

which I'm pacing along. 'That,' you say, pointing and heaving, after finally coming to the top of the small hill. The walk has reduced you to a level of incapacitated panting that is frankly embarrassing. Magnanimously ignoring your pathetic display of fitness, I look to where you are pointing and realise what is perplexing you. 'Oh, *that*.' I smile knowingly and laugh in a slightly obnoxious way that annoys you a little bit but also makes you really respect me and wish you were me. 'That, my dear little city dweller, is open space.'

'Open space' is a concept that can confuse people from the city upon arriving in the countryside. *What's that large patch where the hotels should be?* they wonder. *What is that big blue carpet thing that I see when I look up, which is usually filled with skyscrapers, billboards and neon lights?* Well, that's open space and the sky: don't be afraid. This is what it is *supposed* to be like. Sometimes, we are afraid of open space; its vastness can be terrifying. For most of modern time, we have made it our mission to get rid of as much open space as possible. We see a natural world empty of humanity's fingerprint and, like a toddler who has been handed some crayons and a colouring book, we start filling it in.

To try to help you imagine open space, we will do a thought experiment. Think of the park in the middle of the city where you sometimes eat your lunch. Now, imagine if the whole city was this park and all the other stuff wasn't there. This is what we're dealing with here. When people arrive in the countryside, sometimes the vast lack of man-made things can drive them insane. It's like when tourists land in Paris and discover the chefs aren't controlled by friendly puppeteering rats that live on top of their heads. Not everyone can handle it. Luckily, you're with me and I can explain to you why all is as it should be in the countryside: it is *nature's* way.

Open space is what happens when you just leave things alone. It results in dramatically fewer Starbucks and a huge reduction in car parks. It might seem to you and your untrained eye that there is nothing there. This deep, infinite, perceived nothingness might fill you with anxiety and give you a strong desire to run, jump on a bus back to town and hop into the nearest busy lift and take a deep calming breath in through your nose before realising with disgust that you've accidentally inhaled a fart. Before you do this, I ask you to look again, to gaze out across the hills and the patchwork quilt of the countryside. Look closer and deeper. 'You're looking,' I say to you as you squint out from our vantage point atop the small hill, 'but you're not *seeing*.' You glance at me, impressed by my undeniable wisdom, and with a newfound understanding you look out across the panorama and are reduced to tears as a whole new world is suddenly revealed to you. The seeming emptiness of open space is gone: finally, you see.

What was once a vast, barren place where hotels and competitively priced German supermarkets should be is now filled with grassy knolls, trickling brooks and thick hedgerows, luscious fields, thick forests and a big beautiful blue sky covering it all in a warm, tender embrace. 'Thank you,' you say between sobs of tears, 'for I was blind and now I can see.' I walk towards you and hold your head gently upon my soft yet muscular chest. It seems to you that I am radiating some sort of golden glow. 'Nonsense, my child,' I say. 'All that has passed is that which you have done for yourself.' (Although it's obvious to both of us that I definitely DID do something quite incredible.) 'Now let us walk, for there is so much more I have to show you.' It's at this moment you decide that yes, there definitely is the vague light of a halo gently framing my head.

And with this euphoric moment of epiphany, we walk together down the hill, along the leafy path and into the countryside. You are still trying to keep up with my pace, as it seems I am almost gliding. I speak as we rove, and eagerly, reverently, your ears open wide. Hungry for the truth of my words, you listen.

More blank-space bits

How to describe those green configurations that cover the countryside? What a task, what a task.

Patrick Kavanagh, the celebrated Irish poet, once said it would take a lifetime to know just a corner of a field. For someone who considers themselves a national poet, that is a pretty embarrassing thing to admit. It's a bit of land composed mostly of grass. Was that so difficult, Patrick, really?

But is that all a field is? Isn't it also a mass of luscious grass that deftly camouflages hidden cowpats for the unwitting walker to step in? Or the place where you, as a teenager with nowhere better to go, spent the evening with friends drinking whatever it was you could steal from your parents' liquor cabinet? (If my parents are reading, this is a completely hypothetical analogy.) You see, a field is also a space to *put* things into. Like an empty box, it seems to only hold significance when filled with things. Farmers like filling them up with animals or crops: they hate when fields are empty, it distresses them. 'There's so much empty space,' they cry. 'I need to fill it up with animals or barley or even a few burnt-out tractors. Something, anything, just make the eternal green disappear. It's driving me insane,

I can't sleep at night, it's in my eyes as I dream, can someone please plant some wheat right now!'

Hedges – the eighth wonder of the world

Upon the lining of our roads and paths, a beautiful balance of shrubbery, branches and leaves combine in a piece of collaborative natural art that we have come to know as hedges. Hedges, or hedgerows, are the dividing lines of the countryside, the markers of boundaries. In terms a city dweller might understand: hedges are the bouncers of the natural world, which stand formidable as you try to enter anywhere you're not supposed to be. If you choose to ignore their warning and pass through without permission, you will be punished, by twigs, thorns or the swift whipping of a thin, well-positioned branch.

Any person who has been fool enough to try and slip through a hedgerow has been rightly rewarded with cuts on their legs, bruises on their hips and their nice new coat ripped to pieces.

The hedge maze: you'd have better luck
trying to get into Berghain.

Or, tragically, as in the case of my cousin Simon,
will never be seen again. One day in August,
Simon went out to buy cigarettes; to his eventual
peril, he took his regular fast route through
the hedge to go to the shops. He was last seen
walking towards the impossibly tiny gap in the
hedge. Me and my family spent weeks shouting
at the hedgerow, shining torches at it and asking
him to follow the light, but to no avail: he never

reappeared, the hedge had swallowed him whole. It was a particularly difficult time for the family as the very day Simon disappeared, we found out the family's secret money stash had been stolen, and several of Simon's clothes and a large suitcase had also gone missing. My father wisely mused, 'The only blessing is that Simon wasn't around to see his family's home plundered like this.'

My cousin Simon somehow got stuck at some point walking through this small, practically impenetrable gap and was never seen again.

But hedges are not just the boundaries between land, they are also the centre of activity in the countryside: they are the cities of the countryside. Within them dwell whole species who exist together in differing degrees of harmony; it's where mice hide from rain, birds build their nests; where cats successfully hunt birds and mice, and where whole hedge schools of Catholic children were secretly taught about transubstantiation by undercover priests before Catholic emancipation in Ireland during the 1800s.

[NB: This, specifically, is why I hate fences so much. There is no activity in a fence, it's an ugly sculpture of dead sticks. Nothing lives in them. I mean, you could try to, but you wouldn't last very long. No animals run into fences to hide from the rain, no birds build their nests in them for their family, and if a priest tried to hide a group of Catholic children behind one in nineteenth-century Ireland to teach them about how they should all feel very guilty about most things in their life, he would be spotted and arrested in minutes.]

Hedges are one of the fastest modes of communication that exist today. Don't believe me? Just hear Marvin Gaye talk about the speed with which he found out his partner was cheating on him in his timeless classic, 'I Heard It Through the Grapevine'. Grapevines and hedges alike are the fastest known means of information-spreading on the planet. If you stand beside a hedge for longer than five minutes, you are practically guaranteed to find out some gossip that you weren't supposed to know. It's a scientific fact. Where people gossip is where culture resides, and in the countryside that is beside hedges.

But they are not just the centre of culture. Artistically, they are also something to behold. Hedgerow constructions can stand next to the likes of Monet, Van Gogh and whoever drew Tintin's fringe as some of the greatest examples of high art that humankind has created. Consider the majestic hedge: bushels of leaves, twigs and branches interlinked and woven together – woody browns and dark greens tastefully counterpointing each other – to form a construction of such solidity that arctic winds simply blow past them without their bowing or swaying.

And what of the berries? The ancient fruits that the hedges freely present to the animals of the earth, perhaps by way of apology for prickling them with their thorns. Seamus Heaney had it right when he went on about blackberry-picking. The hedge shall taketh (your jacket or hat) but the hedge shall giveth in return. You can't beat the early-spring blackberry. Delicious little treats, if you can find them. My dad used to gorge on them – he died tragically young of some sort of vicious stomach ulcer. He told me that his dad, who also died tragically young (he bled out through the arse, it was awful), used to eat bucketloads of them.

I have spent years searching for 'the perfect hedge', a mythological, formidable thing of beauty. It is told that it sits tall, at the height of a Dutchman's neck, and thick: nothing wider than a toddler can slip through. As we walk together down the hill and through the valley, you see me glancing left and right in the hopes of spotting it. Then, as we traipse down a clearing between two thickets of bramble, it appears, a luscious beauty of a thing. A veritable piece of natural wonder.

This is essentially pornography.

You realise now that we are not on some simple walk. This is no ordinary day, it is no mere hike, this is a journey, a walkabout, a path towards an inevitable epiphany. This is Moses on the Mount stuff. This is like when you found out white and red Cheddar were the same flavour except one has food dye in it. It's earth-shattering information and you begin to question whether you are ready to take it in. 'Come on,' I say, while looking deep into your soul with my warm, kind and soothing eyes, 'what I must show you next is truly a wonder to behold.'

Stone walling

'Good fences make good neighbours' wrote Robert Frost in his whimsical poem about marking his territory on a New Hampshire farm, 'but a good stone wall will really show them who's boss,' he whispered to himself after putting down his pen.

Stone walls are the way in which we mark the boundary of our land. They're a visually impressive way of saying 'this is my side and that is yours'. You might think them petty and obnoxious, but anyone who has had to share a desk in primary school with a particularly elbowy desk partner knows their vital importance in the countryside. We need stone walls in order to coexist peacefully with our fellow people, otherwise anarchy will ensue.

Stone walls are one of the few things we humans have gotten right. Do not be fooled by the apparent simplicity of their structure. Most don't even use cement: how is that even possible? How do they stay standing? Well, there is a legend that the stone walls between two farms are kept upright by the force of the neighbouring farmers' matching distrust for each other. The suspicion between neighbouring farmers is so potent it becomes a physical gravitational push emitted from both sides of the stone wall, thus pressing it upright perfectly in between the two farmers' land. Where you see stone walls broken, it is an indication that either there is a rare moment of trust between the two farmers and the wall has fallen down, or – more likely – one farmer's distrust has become so powerful and rageful that it has burst through the opposing one's barriers, blasting the stone wall to bits. It is therefore of paramount importance that all distrust in the countryside remains at a healthy equilibrium; too much or too little and all the stone walls will fall.

The Aran Islands, where trust is
virtually non-existent.

Stone walls are one of the architectural wonders of the countryside. Compare them to the monotonous cement walls that fill the suburban world. The small cement structures that separate gardens in urban society are pathetic attempts at boundary-marking:

if I wanted to (and I have, several times), I could vault over my neighbour's wall and steal the cuttings of his roses or indeed cut a bunch of flowers from his flower patch if, say perhaps (and I'm not saying this happened), I forgot to buy flowers for my partner on Valentine's Day.

In an increasingly polarised world, where people are at each other's throats, alienation and loneliness are skyrocketing and anxiety has become the norm, do stone walls still provide a function? Separating us from our fellow person and building barriers where they needn't be? Do they not celebrate humanity's most base tendencies? If so, should I, in a great act of humanity, knock down my neighbour's wall? No, absolutely not. You clearly haven't met Paul.

Fences do *not* make good neighbours

The eighteenth century called: it wants its unsustainable and inefficient methods of marking the boundaries between property back. Fences (I got a bit sick in my mouth just thinking about them) are the great banality of the countryside. It is a crime that a place so bountiful with beauty and nature's delights must have its face scarred with these gangly, bony, lanky objects.

Visual ugliness and tree death aside, fences are also incredibly impractical. If you're trying to keep something out, it's a fat lot of use a fence is going to be. I demonstrate this on the front cover of this book with all the grace of an Olympian gymnast. Fences are easy to get over, under or even through. There is a reason it isn't called the Great Fence of China. Stone walls, now *that* is a way to keep something out. Ever tried to fit through a stone wall? It's impossible. I know this from experience. I once tried to jump head-first through what I thought was a hole in a stone wall, only to wake up several days later in a regional hospital bed being fed porridge through a tube. Stone walls are completely solid; not even a mouse's tear could slip through the gap of a nice stone wall.

Tom Sawyer, along with the help of his white
picket fence, inventing capitalism.

Fences, on the other hand, are practically inviting the casual trespasser. Having a fence outside your house is asking humans or animals to try and surmount it. It's the security equivalent of smearing yourself in honey then kicking a beehive or ringing Winnie the Pooh's doorbell. Put up a fence and you are rolling out the red carpet for any busybodies to come inside. Fences are made to be breached. Imagine the Greeks had shown up to Troy and found the city they were supposed to be laying siege to surrounded by a large picket fence. The only reason they wouldn't have gotten through is that they would have been incapacitated by fits of laughter at the feeble defences of their Trojan enemies.

Pigs, too, are all too wary of fences and their lack of structural integrity. We have all heard the tale of the three little pigs who were historically saved by stone walls only after their properties built with straw and then sticks (in clear violation of contemporary building regulations) were literally blown down by a wolf – an animal, I should add, that is not noted for its blowing capabilities. I implore you, for security purposes, stay away from fences unless you want your home to be invaded by wolves and/or the Greeks.

Trees: don't believe the hype

When people take photos of nature, it's never of the thankless hedges, who do so much unnoticed heavy lifting in the countryside panorama. It's always the trees they notice. Philistine passers-by will get their snap of the old oak tree that has its branches so low you can sit on the lowest one and have a picnic. 'Isn't this lovely? What a picturesque spot. Trees truly are marvels of nature,' you mutter. Meanwhile, in the distance, within earshot, sits the humble hedge, ignored, outcast. Undervalued for far too long, despite its major contributions to the wildlife of the countryside.

Yes, trees are beautiful, but you would be too if you didn't have to support several different species inside you like hedges do. 'I've got a small family of owls living in my trunk,' says the tree. Oh boohoo. Try having a colony of field mice in your shoes, several robin nests on your head, a beehive on your back, an ant colony up your sleeves and seven different varieties of wild flower sprouting out of your arse. All the while providing delicious blackberries for the passing traveller. Hedges are just on a different level to trees and they don't even go on about it. Hedges humbly truck on without asking for thanks or even the occasional photograph of themselves. Trees, on the other hand, demand attention by popping up out of the ground in such a pronounced way it's impossible to ignore them.

There is a certain arrogance to trees that you simply do not get from a hedge. A hedge is a collaborative process, with many different elements coming together to create something beautiful. Trees, on the other hand, are individualistic and attention-seeking. Trees stick out of the ground in the middle of a landscape, like some pathetic social media content creator who has lost his following and fans and decided to become a 'countryside influencer'. Meanwhile, the subtle work of a hedge is barely noticed, even though it adds so much to the landscape around. 'Look at me,' the tree seems to say, 'aren't I so pretty? Please bask in my wondrous beauty.' While the hedge wraps the countryside in a nice leafy hug without so much as a word, like falling into the arms of a lover after a long time apart.

If this fell on someone, it would literally kill them.

Ditches: nature's therapist

We never plan to end up in a ditch. But as life buffets us with its unpredictable twists and turns, it is often the place where we find ourselves. 'I woke up in a ditch,' goes the common phrase. It is always a place you 'end up'. It's never, 'Oh, I'm just on my way to the ditch. Fancy coming along?' 'What ditch? Is there a party? Can I bring friends? Should I bring guacamole or is it going to be one of those situations where everyone thinks to bring guacamole, so we just end up with lots of guac and very little of anything else, feck it, I'll make hummus.' No, ditches exist as the liminal space of the countryside. The space in between the space.

Ditches have a cousin in the city: the gutter. Ditches and gutters are the metaphorical rock bottoms of country and city life. But while the gutter is a harsh, hard and usually quite wet place, the ditch is a soft landing to your emotional crisis. Yes, it can be full of water, but sometimes that's just what we need, a cold-water plunge to get us back on our feet. Ditches exist so there is a place we know if we end up there then things aren't going well and we really need to do something to change it up. Like take up yoga or maybe stop binge-drinking and walking home on your own. Ditches are the cradling arms of the countryside that stand beneath us, ready to catch us at our most vulnerable. Like the netting under trapeze artists, they will bounce us back when we fall to our lowest. It is not a place we should ever aim to go. But I walk through life with more security, safe in the knowledge that, however low I fall, the worst that can happen is I will end up in a ditch, as I have many times before.

You could say I'm headed for a ditch right now. I mean, this whole countryside thing . . . What the hell was the idea there? What am I doing? On this path? Taking you on an imaginary trip through the countryside? Pretending I know what I'm talking about . . . I'm a fool, pathetic, I know it and you know it too . . .

'But what about the rest of our walk, Killian?' you exclaim. 'You haven't told us what to do next. I don't know about mountains! I don't know about the rain or about camping and stargazing. There's so much still to tell me about. Can't you get out of that ditch and we'll forget this ever happened?'

You're absolutely right: there's more for you to learn. Especially for someone as ignorant as yourself. Pure city dweller from top to bottom still. Plenty more to learn. We've barely scratched the surface . . . The ditch can wait for now.

Caught by the river

Brooks are yappers. Ever tried to hold a conversation beside a babbling brook? It's like trying to meditate while someone is hoovering. A babbling brook will interrupt you more than your nerdy boyfriend who keeps sharing subtext and important insights while he is making you watch *Lord of the Rings* for the tenth time, in the hopes you will like it as much as he does. Want to get a brook to shut up? Threaten them with a dam, that tends to work in my experience. Say, for example, you're trying to explain your skincare routine to a friend who is definitely hanging on your every word and some noisy brook won't stop interrupting you while you're explaining the chemical complexity of your cutting-edge French SPF/pH-neutralising combo cream – just start slowly pouring the cement (I forgot to mention you'll need to have several bags of cement in order to pull this off) into the brook and this'll shut it right up. In the interest of conservation and safety, don't *actually* build a dam. That would be a mistake. First of all, you're putting the beavers out of a job – nobody likes a scab – and secondly, brooks are far more powerful and connected than you might think. Behind the innocent trickly brook is an older sibling, the stream, and that older, more frightening sibling has another far older and far more terrible sibling who you should fear and respect with every ounce of your being if you like having dry socks: the river.

Popular music uses rivers as a motif to describe something lazy, something relaxing, something nostalgic yet timeless. Old Man River, messing about on the river, rolling down the river, these popular standards have successfully lulled the masses into viewing rivers as a wonderful benign pleasure that we should enjoy and appreciate. Oh boy is that some successful propaganda from the river. Rivers are to be respected and feared. There is a power within them that can swallow up whole swathes of the countryside on the briefest whim.

I have one consistent rule when going through the countryside and that is: don't mess with rivers. The way waterfalls flop down rock faces can make you think the river's just given up, but don't be sucked in: rivers are the alphas of the countryside; their armies of incels (brooks and streams) who support them feed their mass and give them a power that is not to be messed with. It's a river's world and we're all just living in it.

This woman has no idea the danger she's putting herself in.

Weather warning

There's really only one kind of weather in the countryside, and that is windy. Wind is there to annoy us. It knows this and performs its role admirably. The wind is nature's rascal who gusts across the countryside causing mischief wherever it blows. Relieving yourself by the roadside, are you? How would you like your steady flow to abruptly change in direction so that your own urine sprays backwards onto your trousers, like some sort of reverse golden shower? Thanks, wind, much appreciated. Using an umbrella to stop the rain coming down from the sky and falling onto your head? Hard luck, the rain is now sideways, you figure it out. Cheers, wind, thanks a bunch, at least that washes the pee from my trousers, you're very kind.

Q: Which of these photos have wind in them?
A: Photo 2 (you know there is wind,
because the people are sad).

PART 2

All creatures great
and not-so-great

I've shown you the joys and hazards of the features of the land. Now it is time to educate you in the fauna of the countryside, or animals, to your more basic linguistic understanding. The creatures of the countryside might seem more docile and friendly than the terrifying hippos and lions of the savannah, but don't be deceived by appearances. It's all an act, and the sooner we all wise up to it, the sooner we can save ourselves from imminent destruction at their hands. If you happen to be reading this near or in the company of cattle, be hypervigilant. Make no mistake, the cows are listening.

We need to talk about cattle

Beneath the picturesque veneer of the countryside lies a dormant beast, ready to rise up. That's right: the cow. There are more cows in Ireland than people. But not just cows. Their woolly pals, sheep, too. Sheep match the human population one to one. This raises a very serious question not being covered by mainstream media: what if the national herd were to revolt?

Confidently, I think I could take on two sheep, while potentially outsmarting at least one cow – and I'm not some regular Joe. I'm someone who, through my own deduction, has assessed that I have the strength and mental might to overcome these beasts. We need to keep an eye on farm animals. All it takes is for one Hereford heifer to accidentally sit on its owner before they realise they could squash us any time they wanted to. This is a geopolitical disaster waiting to happen. Do you think farmers are up to the task? The same people who get scared if the sky is red in the morning? Those guys? Really?

We need to take matters into our own hands. We must train for the inevitable day that our national herd turns on us. The day is coming – and sooner than you think. Every pub and community centre must start hosting anti-cow-and-sheep defence classes in the evenings. To avoid animal cruelty, we can practise on the hairiest person in town. Which brings me to my next point: every town must start hosting a hairiest-person competition, with the results being entered into a national database to be printed weekly in the back of newspapers where the cinema listing used to be. Humanity is on the line: we must act now.

I hate to say it because I have historically always been against child labour, but children must be trained in the arts of cow and sheep warfare as well. This is an unfortunate reality of the times we're living in. Children must be taught to travel in packs through fields and mimic the guerrilla techniques employed by various terrorist groups of the past to stage surprise ambush attacks on unsuspecting cows. I'd say seventeen toddlers for every one-tonne cow. Three to distract with melodic song (we know this is the cows' weakness) and the other fourteen to use a complicated pulley system to hoist the cow into a tree using counterweights, rendering the cow immobile. The animals won't be harmed but they will be reminded who is boss.

'Keep your friends close and your enemies closer.'
Sun Tzu, *The Art of War*.

But before we start banging on the doors of the parliament demanding immediate vigilante child bovine-guerrilla groups, let us consider another option. What if we do not fight this war that is facing us? What if we, like Kutuzov in defending Moscow from Napoleon, simply let them take charge? We have had a good shot at running things, us humans; is it now time, like an older sibling tired of hogging the controller, to let someone else have a go? Who knows? It could be better for humans as well as the planet. I've never met a cow I didn't like, and I bet you haven't either. Maybe this will ring in a new era of joy and prosperity. We'll all sit down when it rains, and the land will flow with milk and ~~honey~~ lots of milk. I, for one, bow down to our bovine overlords: take the mantle, dear milk-giving friends. To you, the gentle giants of the countryside, moo-ers of the meadows, creators of cheese, do we bow and submit our servitude. Let the bovine era commence.

Sheep are a different matter. Sheep are protesters, they are activists, they are provocateurs. We use them as a metaphor for the worst, most brainless of our society. Those who follow the crowd, those who mindlessly do as others do without a thought. This characterisation of sheep couldn't be further from the truth, however. They are some of the most thoughtful and deeply individual animals ever to have bounded across a daisy-filled meadow. Sheep are *constantly* staging protests. To you it might look like a herd of sheep blocking the road and stopping you from driving because they've lost their way, but not so! That is an act of civil disobedience that the sheep are staging to protest the several issues they care deeply about.

The West Cork Wool Boycott: widely misinterpreted as a group of sheep misled onto the R586, these sheep were in fact protesting the misuse of their wool by the furry community.

Most outliers and agitators in human history have something of the sheep in them. Che Guevara? I've never seen a bigger sheep of a man – that patchy woollen beard of his, it's pure Scottish Blackface. Socrates? Sure, wasn't he just a shaved Horned Dorset with a nice white tunic on? Sheep live together in harmony and have a plentiful joyous life. This is a result of their strong unions. If we want to move forward as a society, perhaps after all it is to the sheep we must look for guidance.

Or we could just do the gangs-of-kids-attacking-the-cows thing. I genuinely think either of these approaches would work.

Hikers

The road widens and we set up by a fence to rest for a moment (I appreciate this new, revelatory know-ledge about cattle takes time to sink in). The sweet silence is broken by a distant rumbling. 'What's that?' you ask. 'I'm not sure,' I say, frowning. The noise grows steadily. The soft rumbling sounds like the thud of a million tiny hammers. Each second, the noise becomes louder, and soon it is upon us, the bang and slap of leather and rubber on gravel.

'Oh no,' I say, clutching my hand to my chest, 'I thought this path was safe.' I start staggering around, looking for shelter.

'What are you doing? What's that noise? What is happening?' you say, terrified.

The thundering builds to a crescendo and we both crouch in fear. It is just now that vague memories fill your head, of the sound of hundreds of children running down the stairs on the last day of school, the roar of the wildebeest stampede in *The Lion King*, the impending terrifying thunder of an army closing in on its enemy. You look up at me, eyes wide with fear: 'Is that? . . . It can't be . . .' 'Yes,' I shout, my hands over my ears. 'Take cover . . . the hikers are here.'

And here they are. A roving mass of muscular bare legs, heavy hiking boots and colourful fleeces. I shout to you as we shrink behind a wall, like two soldiers sheltering in the trenches. 'Take cover. If they stick to the trail, we might just make it out alive.' The stampede of hikers takes what feels like hours to pass. Like a horde of Vikings, they roll past us ceaselessly. Some occasionally stop to take a swig of water from a reusable beaker and put their hands on their hips and say 'Ahhhh, now, isn't this *nice*', before rejoining the blurry, multicoloured train of hikers. And just like that, they are gone. We both stand, shakily, holding our heads, the noise still ringing in our ears. We sit next to each other on a stone, staring out at the disappearing cloud of dust. You bow your head and weep. I let you lean on my shoulder. 'It's OK, they're gone, you're going to be all right.' My face, however, shows the raw truth: while they are out there, none of us is safe.

Hiking groups have become more and more powerful in the last few years. Membership has skyrocketed. Gangs of them patrol the hills every morning on the weekends. Clad in Lycra and fleeces, they trample over picnic blankets and children's birthday parties without regard. When they reach a village, it's like the community is under siege. Coffee shops have started closing their shutters in the hopes that they'll just pass by, but they never do. Nothing will stop a red-faced hiker from getting an oat-milk flat white after a morning hike. Have you ever had to use a café bathroom after forty hikers have gone in after their post-morning-hike coffee? Trust me, it's not pretty.

This is a global problem. Hikers have become a sort of wandering mercenary army that threatens to upheave political stability. Once, a large group of hikers called the Nifty Over Fifties did the Camino and swelled to such a size that they became one of the most powerful voting blocks in Spain. They ran the country for a while, rewriting the constitution to include hiking as one of Spain's core tenets. It reached a point where the Crown Prince of Spain was forced to go on bended knee to the leader of the Nifty Over Fifties. The UN called it the most significant threat to Spanish democracy since the days of General Franco. They eventually agreed to withdraw only when Spain promised a permanent price freeze on Lycra. There's nothing we can do to stop them, they're too powerful. It's best to just close your eyes and hide when they pass by, and be glad they're only around once a week.

Susan, Mildred and Jessica leading the
advance on Catalonia.

The good people

We walk through a forest and come across a large pile of stones. I steer you wide of it without saying a word. 'What's that?' you say. 'Nothing,' I answer tersely, 'just a pile of old stones. Come on, let's keep moving.' 'Wait,' you say, 'one of those stones kind of looks a bit like Jason Statham's head!' 'Most stones look like Jason Statham's head, let's keep moving.' 'No, this one really has the right shape. I feel like I'm watching a mid-tier action movie just looking at it, I'm going to pick it up.' As you move towards the pile and reach out, I grab your hand. 'Don't do it!' 'Why?' you reply, astonished by the strength of my grip. 'It's just a stone.'

Oh the naivety. 'It's not just a stone, that's a faerie fort.' You laugh and once again you reach out to take the stone, but in a flurry of movements that wouldn't look out of place in, well, a Jason Statham movie, you find yourself lying on your back on the floor. 'Don't touch the faerie fort.'

Faerie forts and all manner of things otherworldly are littered all over the countryside. They are to be respected and avoided. I'm not saying they are real. Not at all. I am saying, why bother finding out if they're real or not? What good does it do you to mess with something and find out in the worst possible way that they are? Pick up a stone that looks like your favourite bald celebrity, bring it home and show it to your friends, put it on your mantelpiece. Wake up the next day to find you now smell pungently of garlic and no matter how much you wash, it won't go away. That's the kind of mischief they can get up to. They can turn your hands into your feet and your feet into your hands. They can make your arse your face and your face your arse.

And what do they look like? Think jockeys. Small and unassuming. Humans, but a little bit slighter. Like jockeys, you wouldn't trust them for a second. The kind of thin frame that if I brought one of them home to my house, my mother would spend the entire time just trying to feed them as much food as possible (like the French exchange student in secondary school: 'Are you sure you don't want more mash, Marcel? There's plenty of gravy there and you've barely touched your boiled ham, here, let me cut it up for you . . .').

It's their eyes that give them away. There are plenty of people in popular culture who are suspected of being of the Sidhe, the ancient race of faerie folk. Cillian Murphy, for example, the small man from Cork with a beautiful big head and clear blue eyes: that's a faerie. Indeed, having a massive face and vivid eyes – one of the key attributes of the faeries – also seems to be what's needed in order to be a Hollywood actor. So it's no wonder there has been an explosion of Irish actors in Hollywood over the years. Most, if not all, are not people but actually faeries getting their moment on the red carpet. Saoirse Ronan, the way she can slip between accents at the drop of a hat and change her image with ease: that's a faerie. Daryl McCormack, those are the eyes of an ancient supernatural being. Paul Mescal, however, is not one, judging by the metrics of his head and bulky physique: that is a pure, potato-fed Kildare man.

Be careful when you wander home through the countryside, especially at night. There are too many stories of wayward drunks wandering home from the pub, leaning to pee on what they thought was a pile of old stones only for it to turn out to be a gateway to another realm. These poor souls end up being cursed with the eternal sensation of needing to sneeze but never actually being able to. Faeries are creative in their curses, and much like hipsters (it's quite possible the two groups are linked), irony seems to be their main weapon. They'll make a French person allergic to butter, a sailor will lose their sea legs, dancers will be given two right feet, doctors will be made to gag at the sight of blood, people who work in sales will be made allergic to cocaine.

Barry Keoghan doesn't even pretend to be human.

Tread carefully – it might all be true, it might all be complete nonsense. But why be the one who finds out? You leave them alone and they'll leave you alone, that's how I've gone about it and I've ended up just fine, right?

Farmers who lean on fences ...

We come upon a small village square filled to the brim with farmers, each of them with a small bit of wheat sticking out of their mouth, a keystone feature of the countryside. In the centre of the large group of disgruntled-looking farmers is a man standing on a milk crate with a megaphone in his hand. He is straining to speak over the hum of chatter and the occasional heckle of the unruly group surrounding him. 'This is something very special to see,' I inform you. 'It's the annual meeting of the National Association for Farmers who Lean on Fences with a Bit of Wheat Stuck Lazily in their Mouth.' 'The national association of what?'

'Have you ever heard of someone being in the

countryside and turning a corner and coming upon a nice farmer leaning casually on a fence with a cheerful smile and a little bit of wheat stuck lazily in their mouth?''Yes, of course,' you say, exasperated, 'but I thought that was by chance.' 'Nothing is by chance,' I say, tapping my nose, 'everything is carefully crafted. Now watch, this is the meeting where they decide who gets to go where.'

The man on the milk crate – who is called Barnie, if the heckles are anything to go by – has become frustrated with the crowd:

'Now if I could please just take a bit of your time for a few short announcements,' he shouts at the crowd, a little too loudly. 'It is in my capacity as the chairperson of the National Association for Farmers who Lean on Fences with a Bit of Wheat Stuck Lazily in their Mouth to . . .'

'Has the meeting officially begun?' a neatly dressed farmer interrupts. 'If so, as health and safety officer for the National Association for Farmers who Lean on Fences with a Bit of Wheat Stuck Lazily in their Mouth, it's my duty to read out the mission statement and go through the safety precautions and guidelines for wellness . . .' This is interrupted with a collective groan and heckling before the megaphone restores order.

'That's enough,' shouts Barnie, 'we can do that later, right now we have a few important points of order. As I'm sure most of you are aware, the recent spike in membership has started to cause a lot of issues within our ranks. Just last week in Tipperary, we had four farmers leaning with a bit of wheat stuck lazily in their mouths on the same fence, it looked ridiculous. Now, hands up, four farmers on one fence: that's on us, it was a clerical error from the coordination department, but this kind of thing is only going to keep happening. People have started asking questions. Some have had the gall to say that we farmers have too much time on our hands.'

The crowd gasps in disapproval.

'Do they know how early we get up?' shouts a red-faced man.

'That's it,' shouts an athletic-looking woman at

the back of the crowd, 'I've had enough. No more eggs for anyone!'

Barnie calms them again. 'No. No more egg strikes. The last one almost caused the stock markets to crash. We need to deal with this in a way that suits everyone. We're simply going to have to find extra space for us to lean on fences.' 'It's already out of hand,' John Joe pipes up. 'I spent the whole of last year stationed behind a wall. Nobody could see me. It was pointless. If you're going to spend all day lazing on a fence with a long bit of grass in your mouth, you want people to see you. That's why we do it.'

'If a farmer leans on a fence in the countryside with a bit of wheat hanging out the side of their mouth,' the safety officer muses, 'but there's nobody there to see them, does it really happen?' This is met with a sudden stillness as the farmers reflect on the philosophical offering. Barnie brings them back to business:

'Myself and the others on the organising committee have had a word with a few higher-ups in the Ordnance Survey and they're willing to find us the space we need by "discovering" some prime real estate around the edges of the national parks map. In return, we supply them with free Cheddar for life.' This is met with cheers all around.

'OK. That's settled. The next point of order, again with the swell in numbers for the National Association for Farmers who . . .' He mumbles the rest and continues, 'there simply isn't enough wheat to go around, we're on the brink of a national bread shortage. Now I know this won't be popular, but myself and the committee have been looking into using barley replacements or even – and this is really an interesting idea – reusable wooden wheat to be more environmentally friendly.' This is met with a large outburst of rage from the crowd.

I grab your arm and pull you away. 'Quickly, let's get out of here, this could get ugly.' We turn around and start walking away just as John Joe and a group of bearded Kerrymen topple Barnie's milk cart and unsuccessfully attempt to wrestle the megaphone out of his hand. Before long, the riot that engulfs the entire village is just a gentle hum on the breeze behind our backs.

(Dis)Content creators

We reach a particularly picturesque spot beside a lake. An excited look creeps across my face. 'Just look at this view, it's perfect.' I take off my backpack and pull out a tripod, which I set up just by the edge of the lake. Fixing my cameraphone on to the tripod, I turn to you:

'Can you help with this? It won't take a moment, then we can keep going.'

'What's going on here?' you say, confused.

'Content creation, obviously. You now know that I am the leading voice on all things countryside, but the rest of the world *doesn't* know that yet. For me to make my big comeback, I need content to let the world know of my rebirth as a prophet of rural life. Like Jesus, but obviously less problematic.' I walk in front of the camera. 'Come on, you work the camera.'

Content shot:

Standing beside the lake with eyes closed, wind blowing hair, then eyes open with shock. 'OK,' I say, 'caption that one "when you're meditating in nature and you suddenly realise the entire day has gone by".' 'But you weren't meditating,' you say, confused. 'Yes, I know that, but I could have been. I've done it before,' I explain. 'Really? Have you?' 'Well, no,' I reply shortly. 'But as I said, I could if I wanted to. Please. I need this.'

Content captured:

Killian chops wood topless while slapping the wood more times than necessary beforehand.

Killian sits cross-legged by the side of the lake and meditates. Caption reads, 'Most people my age are out partying and living pointless lives while I'm literally beside a lake meditating trying to find inner peace lol follow for more #innerpeace #follow4more.'

Killian does yoga on the edge of the lake.
Caption: 'I actually can't vinyasa flow properly any more unless I'm beside a lake but that's just me I guess lol #follow4more #innerpeace.'

Killian sits beside lake with laptop, caption reads, 'Nice "office" for the day crying laughing smiley emoji.'

Killian looks around with wonder and accidentally bumps into a tree, then laughs. Caption: 'When you're so taken in by the beauty surrounding you that you accidentally bump into a tree loooool follow for more funny content #follow4more #innerpeace #funnynaturevideos.'

Killian walking beside the lake. Caption: 'POV: You're walking beside the lake.'

You frown. 'But, Killian, if you're creating fake poses, chasing likes and not actually living by the laws of the countryside, what is the point of all of this?' I'm not sure I appreciate your tone, so I decide it's time to introduce you to the ways of the locals, to put you in your place.

PART 3
Do it like a local

Now you have familiarised yourself with the countryside and the animals that you will find there, you are becoming more and more at one with the environment. The next step is blending in with the rest of the people who live here. Becoming more local than the locals themselves, as I have successfully done. I've become so inconspicuous that locals affectionately refer to me as 'bog Scarlet Pimpernel'.

How to communicate with countryfolk

The path finally grows flat and we come to an easy, straight country road with an island of grass lining the middle. It is here that we see, in the distance, the small figure of a woman on a bicycle cycling towards us. She is going at a slow pace and as she reaches us, I make a gesture you've never seen before: I flick my head down and up, then murmur a vague noise. In response, the woman on the bicycle lifts up one of her fingers on the left hand while holding the handle and mimics a slight nodding of her head, before continuing onwards. Not a word is shared between us, but as we reach a fork in the trail, I take us along the left route.

'I'd usually take you along the right,' I explain, 'but that woman there just said there's a river that has flooded the path.' You turn to me, perplexed. 'What do you mean, she *said*? That woman who passed? She didn't utter a word.' 'Ah yes,' I reply pityingly. 'Though you clearly did not understand it, what you just witnessed was a country conversation.'

We people of the countryside have long evolved past the need for verbal communication. We have developed a non-verbal mode of communication that has such nuance and subtlety it has become the preferred mode of socialising. Think back: have you ever walked into a country pub and been taken aback at how silent it was, even though it was filled with people sitting next to each other? You might have thought they were sitting silently, but those people in the pub were speaking, just not with words. The unfortunate reality is, if you didn't hear them speaking, they were almost certainly talking about you. And not in a good way.

Finger raises, nods and winks are the preferred gestures by which sentences are communicated. The less movement involved in the gesture, the better. I once witnessed two older gentlemen sit beside each other outside a cottage and have an hours-long meaningful discussion on the properties of subatomic particles without anything more than the merest raising of an eyebrow between them. There is not much scientific analysis done on this particular anthropological wonder, but from my own observations I believe it to have originated from the deep desire and need to talk about city people directly in front of them, without those people realising.

It's a language that is learned only by living it. No book has been written and no translations can be found. It is something you will only ever understand by living the authentic country life. I have, however, managed to translate a few basic gestures to help you, the basic city dweller, avoid abject humiliation:

> Raising a finger: 'How are you and how is your family?'
> Raising a finger (but quickly this time): 'All is well and good with me and how is yourself?'
> A slow half-raising of a finger: 'Can you believe Arsenal's performance on the weekend? If they don't sort out their defence, you can kiss goodbye to a title challenge.'

Of course, this non-verbal way can seem problematic to those city dwellers used to the perceived efficiency of a verbal-based system of communication. The non-verbal method is more about understanding a person and not the specifics of what they said. The vagueness allows a certain nuance that is lacking in most contemporary conversation. I know some people from the countryside who haven't said more than a few phrases for several decades. Words themselves are decreasing in popularity at an accelerating pace. Except, of course, when it comes to local gossip. Country people love gossip more than a shepherd loves a red sky at night. For some things, we need language, and one of those things is explaining who looked hungover in Mass on Sunday and did you see the hour they went crawling home at? For that, names, dates and graphic details are vital.

This is married couple John and Mary, who haven't spoken a word to each other in forty-seven years.

The Country Shop

At some point along this walk, I realise you need food and a warm cup of tea to build you up for the rest of our morning's ramble through the countryside. But where can we find such a place to satisfy these needs? There is one such marvel: the local Country Shop.

No stretch of countryside is complete without a small shop to serve the needs of its locals and passing travellers. The Country Shop is quite a particular place: rustic on the outside and tiny on the inside. Despite its small stature, it must also have nearly everything a human could imaginably need, from fresh milk to old Phillips screwdrivers that are no longer manufactured, from Scart cables, seventieth birthday cards and out-of-date KitKats to dusty old DVDs of *Pride and Prejudice* (the Colin Firth one). The country shop will have one and only one of each of these things.

'Two types of every animal onto the ark,' said

God to Noah, as the winds started to pick up and the clouds turned dark. 'Oh, and one type of absolutely everything to go in the tiny country shop,' he added. Noah, used to God's antics, just sighed and rolled his eyes.

As for the pricing in this miraculous place, that is fixed on by the shopkeeper to be whatever the hell they want. That tin of beans? It's three times what you'd usually pay. That singular tomato? Half the usual price. Why? Because they feel like it. See that pound-shop-quality flashlight you desperately need because it's dark and the power just went out in the country cottage you have rented in order to flee the pressures of city life? That'll be a mark-up of ten times the price, you complete and absolute gobshite. Oh, what's that? You aren't happy with the shocking prices they have set for you? Well, tough, there is absolutely nothing you can do about it!

They have you right where they want you. You are in the pocket of the local shopkeeper and there's nothing you can do about it except smile gratefully and thank your lucky stars they aren't charging you more.

Who are these mythical shopkeepers anyway? They are special, ancient people who will take as many minutes from your day as they possibly can.

Let's say you are hurriedly buying some plasters for your child, who has cut themselves on a prickly bush. Sorry, the sloth-like movements of this ancient shopkeeper will have you tearing your hair out with frustration. Plus, you don't have cash, so they have to whip out an old card machine, but the shopkeeper can't seem to find the right cable needed to connect it to the dial-up modem. Then your card won't work because the signal is dodgy. All the while, they're rambling on happily about how this winter is a lot warmer than previous winters and how, back in their day, the taps in the kitchen wouldn't work for the chill in the mornings. Meanwhile, as you're tamping down the growing impatience you can feel bubbling up inside, you realise your child has just outright collapsed and now you must go to hospital all because you didn't have the heart to tell the sweet old-timer to shut the f*** up and give you the plasters.

We walk into the shop together and smile at the shopkeeper, who is twisting an old radio trying to get a signal of some horse race that is happening in some far distant land. We pour ourselves two teas from the rickety coffee machine that looks less like a dispenser of beverages and more like a villain from the early *Doctor Who* episodes. We go to the counter and pay the shopkeeper in cash, and he slowly counts out the change while telling us that his grandson has a tip on a horse in the two fifteen at Leopardstown (Smart Charming Baby), and for you to not take the hilly pass because a tree fell down in the wind last week. Before his monotonous small talk lulls us into a sleep from which we never awaken, I shout, 'What's that behind you?' As the shopkeeper slowly turns, we sprint out of the shop to freedom.

The blow-ins

We pass a picturesque-looking farmhouse with a lot of commotion outside. A tractor is doing doughnuts while a perplexed-looking man chaotically attempts to regain control behind the wheel. A woman in high heels and a pair of white trousers is shrieking hysterically while walking carefully through a muddy paddock, trying to feed some pigs. A young boy is chasing a group of distressed sheep, while his gothic teenaged sister is walking around a field, holding her phone aloft and complaining about the lack of internet service.

You look at me in confusion: 'What's going on here?'

'That,' I say, with a solemn look on my face, 'is the Mulhern family. They're participating in one of those TV shows where they get a family from the city and have them run a farm in the countryside for a year.'

'But why?' you ask.

'Why? Because there's nothing the public likes more than watching a suburban family struggle with the daily difficulties of running a farm. These shows are incredibly popular. BBC, Channel 4, RTÉ, ITV, Netflix – who knows, it could be any of them behind this one. Most farms you see in the countryside have at some stage been run by a suburban family who have had their trials and tribulations filmed and broadcast for public consumption.'

'That seems like it would get boring and formulaic after a while,' you suggest.

'Formulaic? You obviously haven't seen a teenaged boy from the city try and stream the Champions League final on rural Wi-Fi. It never gets old. Come on . . .' We walk over towards the farm and sit on a nearby bench with a full view of the farmhouse. 'Let's watch for a while.' Within earshot, a man with a sardonic Geordie accent narrates the unfolding chaos:

It's five past ten and Mr Mulhern hasn't even got the tractor working yet. Mrs Mulhern is trying to feed the pigs but they don't seem to be interested in the pork chops she's made them. 'That's pig meat!' little Johnny shouts from across the field as he chases the sheep. 'You can't feed pig meat to pigs, it'll make them go crazy.' Too late, however, as one of the larger pigs, Benny, has taken a bite into one of the garlic-glazed pork chops Mrs Mulhern woke at 5 a.m. to cook and suddenly his pupils shrink to dots and he starts squealing and tearing around the paddock with a crazed look in his eyes. He bashes into Mrs Mulhern, who falls onto the muddy ground, ruining her nice white jeans. Hopefully, it'll come out in the wash. Mr Mulhern screams from the out-of-control tractor, which is still spinning in circles. 'Susan, just lie there and pretend to be dead,' he shouts. In an attempt to save his wife from the crazed pig, he leaps out of the tractor cockpit, narrowly escaping being crushed by one of the tractor's wheels. He lands heavily into the muddy paddock next to his wife. Benny the pig pauses his galloping and turns to Mr and Mrs Mulhern lying in the mud. He starts aggressively snorting, readying to charge. 'Why is there no internet in this shithole?' Jenny shouts from the field, waving her phone around. 'I've been trying to watch the new Kardashian apology video for accidentally inciting

*a violent mob at the GoPro store for the last three hours.'
'Jenny,' little Johnny says, pointing at the pig pen, 'I
think the pig is going to attack them.' Benny snarls and
starts galloping towards Mr and Mrs Mulhern as they
try to help each other out of the sticky mud. Will Benny
the cannibal-crazed pig take a few chunks out of the
Mulherns? Will Susan get the mud out of her white
Simone Rocha jeans? Will Kourtney Kardashian serve
prison time for her role in the Ohio GoPro Riots? Find
out next week on* Honey, We Bought a Farm!

The aftermath of *Honey, We Bought a Farm!*,
Channel 4, 9 p.m.

'My God,' you say, sitting on the bench as we share a box of popcorn together, 'this is absolutely brilliant.'

What to wear?

People don't respect nature's need for the right costume and apparel. If I had it my way, large, bald German bouncers would stand beside a velvet cord and only allow people access to the countryside if they have the correct attire. It would be like an exclusive Berlin nightclub except with less leather, to avoid distressing the cows.

You see, the trails and roads of the countryside are, in fact, catwalks of fashion to rival those of Paris and Milan. You may think that nobody is going to see you and therefore what you wear doesn't matter, but you couldn't be more wrong. What you wear matters deeply, for many reasons.

Firstly, people *will* see you. One thing I've learned about the countryside is that even though you didn't see anyone, that doesn't mean they didn't see you. The communication network in rural communities passes like a whispering wind. As we've previously discussed, they don't even require language to pass on information. You might think, as you're leaving the house, 'Oh, I'll put on this old coat and that woolly hat that I got for Christmas, nobody is going to notice if I don't look like Beyoncé during my Sunday-morning walk.' Newsflash, someone will spot you and soon everyone will know; news travels like lightspeed in the countryside. Even Beyoncé will know. News of a mismatched outfit worn in the morning could be on Beyoncé's desk by the afternoon, the rest of Destiny's Child will know by the evening, you'll be the talk of the town. Is this what you wanted? Three American women making fun of you while singing in perfect harmony and dancing tight choreography?

The other reason what you wear matters is practicality. Nature has a habit of trying its best, when you are in it, to make you uncomfortable. It has three main ways of doing this, by making you either cold, sore or, worst of all, wet. When you tog up in the countryside, it is important to avoid all those three things by dressing appropriately for whatever weather or geographical environment you happen to be in. This, in many ways, is what sets the catwalks of the countryside ahead of the esteemed ones of New York, London and Mulhuddart. The models in their outfits on those runways simply have to look striking, artistic and beautiful. They don't have to worry, while walking down the runway wearing their conceptual outfits constructed entirely of bubbles and ideas, that the heavens will open upon them and render their clothing obsolete. In the countryside, this is a major factor to contend with.

You cannot hike in flips-flops; Crocs also are out (a universal, not just in the countryside). All clothing is required to be both permeable and waterproof, defying all known laws of physics. Jackets should have a thousand pockets. Every time you pick up your walking jacket, you should find something in a pocket that you thought you'd lost: a toffee, a leaking ballpoint pen, lots of tissues, your partner's sunglasses that you insisted you didn't borrow and haven't seen anywhere. Don't wear that favourite pair of jeans that make your arse look great because very soon they will be covered in so much mud it'll look like you had an accident. White is a no-no for obvious reasons and so too is black: too French. The only colours allowed are brown, green and, in some rare instances, blue. Bear in mind that if you wear blue, especially a light-coloured blue, everyone will raise their eyebrows and mutter, 'Well, don't they think they're something special.' My advice would be to stay away from blue, you're not ready for it yet. Start with brown and work your way up.

Take in the air

I'm no mystic man. There isn't a drop of New Age in me. I don't believe in voodoo, or mushrooms curing cancer; astrology is a load of mumbo-jumbo, India simply does not exist. That being said, if there was one health fad that I was to stick my two cents behind, it would be the supreme healing powers of good old country air.

'Fresh air', as your mother calls it when she pulls open the windows in your bedroom at an ungodly hour in the morning after you've had a few too many pints, is a healing elixir. There is nothing quite like that first shock of fresh country air you get when you open the car door after having driven from the city. Previously, your poor lungs have been choking on the putrid urban air. That city stuff is air in name only. If you were to break down the contents of a single breath of city air, you'd be shocked to see how little air is actually contained in each lungful. City air is 28 per cent car fumes, 20 per cent bins, 6 per cent cigarette smoke, 8 per cent vape smoke, 10 per cent sticky floors, 6 per cent chipper, 2 per cent curry sauce, 4 per cent bad breath, 5 per cent farts, 10 per cent nitrogen, 1 per cent oxygen. Fresh country air, on the other hand, consists of 100 per cent fresh country air (plus an admittedly healthy dollop of cow farts and manure).

When you arrive in the countryside after your poor lungs have been consuming garbage fumes for months, then you take a lungful of fresh air, the healing that takes place is immediate. The electric feeling as a breath ful of country air zips its way all around your airways and fills you with a hitherto unknown level of energy simply cannot be matched in city life.

But with every high comes a warning: do not get addicted to this wonderful gift of nature. I've seen too many get lost in the chase of its natural high. It starts with a nice breath of fresh air but soon that is not enough. Sunrise hikes develop into freshwater swimming, but then the water is never cold enough, so ice baths follow. Then they start jumping from steaming hot saunas to icy baths with ever-increasing speed till their skin starts to turn red with bewilderment. Then they get strangers (usually bearded Scandinavians) to lead them in breathing exercises that seem to involve very little actual breathing. After that they get chased by 'wellness experts' who whip at them using leafy branches with the accuracy of a musketeer. But that is not enough. Soon, they will be walking around barefoot at all times. Their boss calls them in, asks them to stop burning sage in the office as they had to call the fire service three times this week and their crystals keep getting stuck in the printer and while they appreciate the desire to do a digital detox, they haven't answered any emails in weeks and the company has lost a significant amount of income from the sales opportunities missed. They lose their jobs and friends get tired of looking at your feet and suddenly no matter how many times you douse yourself in ice-cold water, it won't be enough. Eventually, they leave society and head to some remote part of the wilderness to live an isolated life as a hermit in a small hut.

That said, I have started a small business selling jars full of country air, at a very reasonable price too. Message me if you're interested.

Fiver a pop and there's plenty more
where they came from.

PART 4
Welcome, country dweller!

We have reached the point where I have taught you almost everything I know. Your spiritual journey is almost complete. All that's left is for you to run free in the countryside on your own and see how you get on. If you are ready, you will be tasked with completing the final test. Then and only then will you be considered a true expert of the countryside. But first . . .

The reel life

We come to a small river. I hand you a fishing rod. 'Now fish,' I command. 'But you haven't taught me how.' You take a step back and don't take the rod. 'I'm not ready.' I push the rod towards you again. 'Fish,' I repeat firmly. Your hands tremble as you take the rod. 'This is something you have to do on your own, I can't help, you're on your own,' I say, before turning and walking away. You stand for a moment, then turn to the river and walk close to the edge. 'Careful of the river, you fool! Have you learned nothing?!' a bush that's definitely not me offering helpful advice shouts at you from behind. You jump back from the river with a fright.

What follows next is a complete debacle. You unwind the fishing line and try flicking it into the river, but without a weight it just falls slowly onto the ground in front of you. Fumbling, you tie a stone to the line and try to cast it again, but the line isn't long enough so it swings in a large circle over your head and boomerangs back towards you. The stone whacks you in the stomach. You hunch over in pain. Finally, you cast it out into the river and wait a couple of seconds before getting frustrated at the lack of bites; you reel it in again and cast it further, again waiting a brief second before getting frustrated and reeling it in again. You try casting it further out, but it gets caught in a tree above your head; you try pulling it out of the tree but it's well and truly stuck. Panicking now, you start reeling it in, but this only pulls the branch closer to you, creating a tension between you and the branch. You keep winding with shaking hands; the tension grows. Your feet lift slightly off the ground as you wind yourself up towards the tree. Finally, the tension grows too much, the fishing line snaps and you tumble backwards onto the ground in a heap. 'No, no, no,' I say, coming out from behind the bush, 'that is not how you fish.'

Fishing doesn't really have very much to do with actual fishing. It is just a picnic in disguise. Think about it: when you fish, what do you bring with you? A nice basket with a flask of tea and some sandwiches. When you are fishing, what do you actually spend most of your time doing? That's right, standing, or indeed sitting, beside a river, drinking tea and eating sandwiches. It is entirely possible – in fact, it is extremely common – to spend an entire day fishing without catching any fish. If you spend several hours beside a river sitting on a blanket eating a sandwich drinking tea and having the occasional biscuit, ignoring the stick with a bit of string floating in the water, you have just engaged with the act of having a picnic – and arguably, with the act of fishing.

Most countryside pursuits are picnics in disguise. Hiking? What do you do when you get to the top of the hill? Yes, eat a sandwich. Hiking is just having a picnic in a more scenic location. Swimming? That's an aqua picnic, though be sure to have your picnic post-swim for fear of drowning after eating a particularly heavy sourdough. Shooting? Picnic plus guns. Blackberry-picking is a DIY picnic. Rock climbing? Climb to the picnic. Cross-country running? Last one to the picnic is a rotten egg. Kite flying is actually an ancient mode of communicating long distance to neighbouring communities to say, 'Hey, we're having a picnic over here.' Whenever anyone asks you if you want to do anything in the countryside, the most important thing to bring is a blanket and some sandwiches. If you want to be a real pro, a flask of tea and some biscuits.

All you need is love (and the basic laws of physics)

A small puddle in the middle of the path provides us with a reason to pause. You are tired from the long day's strolling but it's the sort of tired that's earned. The kind of tired that makes lying on the couch and watching countless episodes of the new Australian reality TV show where they get children to plan the parents' wedding feel like a deserved activity. Your muscles and bones ache, but in a pleasant way. The kind of smug pleasant tired that makes you say things like, 'Oh I couldn't possibly, I've been out all day,' or 'I could drop at any moment.' You look into the puddle and see a reflection of yourself smiling back. 'You are ready,' I nod, 'the last vestiges of city dweller have left your body. You're now mostly a countrysider, you're ready to go off on your own.' 'But I'm not ready,' you howl, 'what happens if I don't know what to do?' 'Just think, *what would Killian do?* and you'll be fine.' With that, you start slowly walking away from me. Then you start running.

You breeze through the landscape with ease. Almost floating. The open space no longer fills you with the dread that it did before. 'I hate hotels!' you shout at the top of your lungs. 'Multilevel car parks should be transformed into multilevel fields so as to maximise the amount of field.' 'My God,' I whisper to myself, watching you with jealous wonder, 'I didn't even think of that, you're a natural.'

You walk to a row of saplings and without hesitation bend one over your knee, cracking the spine of the youthful tree. 'What are you doing?' I shout. 'Have you gone completely mad?' But without pause you bend the next sapling over your knee and intertwine it with the following sapling, till the whole line of trees is knitted together in a long, tall, bushy row. 'Is that . . . ?' I hesitate as tears start flooding my eyes. 'It can't be . . .' I fall to my knees, trembling, and sob heavily. At this moment, Edwin van der Sar, former Netherlands international, walks by your construction. 'Shoulder height of an average Dutchman,' I say, awestruck.

'It's a hedgerow, the most beautiful I've ever seen. The perfect hedge. It's more perfect than I ever could have possibly imagined.'

Next, you start placing flat stones on top of each other between us, slowly building a wall. 'Be careful,' I say, 'you're not ready, surely they will fall.' You ignore me and keep laying the stones at lightning speed, placing them tightly together like an expert Tetris player, but the blocks don't disappear. Suddenly, there is a perfect picturesque stone wall between us. 'But it isn't falling?' I say. 'Does this mean we don't trust each other?' 'No,' you reply, 'I realised the secret: it's not distrust that stops the stone walls from falling over – think about it, the answer is right in front of you.' I look over the stone wall at your imploring face and suddenly the answer rushes to my mind: 'It's love, all the walls are kept up by farmers' mutual love for each other.' I jump up, filled with delight at this revelation, gasping in wonder. 'No . . .' you say, 'it's the gaps between the stones. It lets the wind pass through, so they don't blow over.' I look across the stone-wall-filled horizon. 'It's all kept up because of love,' I whisper quietly to myself.

The final test

'Before you can truly be considered one with the countryside, you must first pass the final test,' I declare: 'to speak with a local without them becoming suspicious that you're from the city.'

As I say this, a man walks up to us. He shuffles along the path and takes us in. 'Are you an O'Reilly from up the road?' he says, staring in our direction. 'No, I'm not actually from around here,' I say. 'I know I walk and talk like a local, I fit right in in many respects. You look at me and you probably think, there's a man who was reared in these hills, there's a man who walks, talks and breathes countryside . . .' 'No, not you,' says the man, interrupting me, 'I meant you.' He points past my face, directly at you.

'Oh,' you stutter, embarrassed but also irritatingly pleased, 'no, I'm not an O'Reilly. This is my friend

Killian, he was just showing me around.' The old man laughs. 'Sure why would he be showing you around, that man looks like he hasn't spent five minutes off his phone in the last ten years. That's the face of someone who didn't learn to drive till he was in his late twenties because he grew up around public transport.'

'I'm not going to stand here and be insulted like this,' I say coldly. 'How dare you say that to me?'

'So you didn't learn to drive in your late twenties?' he replies.

'That's beside the point. I belong in the countryside, everyone around here has accepted me as a local.'

'Oh, is that so?' he says with a coy knowingness that makes my blood boil. 'So you wouldn't be that influencer chap, would you?' he says.

'Yeah, that's him,' you say, delighted.

Sensing a disconcerting camaraderie between the two of you, I change my tone. 'Guys, this has all been very pleasant, but I think we need to get on.'

'You're not the fella who lives in the van outside

Mairead's house and teaches her young lad German?' he says, ploughing on.

'What?' you say, shocked. 'You told me you were living in a country cottage and that it had been in your family for generations.'

'A van is just a type of cottage when you think about it,' I stammer.

'Except for the lack of a fireplace,' says the man. 'Or any other aspect that would make it cottagelike,' you add.

'Why exactly are you still here?' I say to the man. I pull on your arm. 'Listen, let's get out of here. This guy clearly doesn't know what he's talking about. I think . . .' – I tap the side of my head – 'he's not exactly all there.'

The man laughs. 'The first week he got here, he ended up getting stuck in Byrne's field back there and Mairead's son had to pull him out with a tractor, him all crying and covered in mud. He gets lost all the time.'

'Seriously?!' you exclaim.

'You take that back right now,' I shout, my face

red with embarrassment. 'I don't get lost, I'm a proper countrysider, it's who I am, it's all I have.'

I fall to my knees. You both look at me sympathetically. 'I think I'd best be off,' the man nods. He walks five paces past us, pulls out his phone and puts it to his ear. 'You'll never guess who I'm after bumping into, that influencer fella, prancing around like he knows what's what. He was with one of the O'Reillys, well they said they weren't an O'Reilly but I'd know that thick forehead anywhere . . . Yeah, it's not brain in there, I reckon it's mostly skull.'

'You know we can still hear you,' I shout at him. He turns quickly then lowers his voice, still completely audible. 'I think they might have heard that there, anyway, how are you getting on?'

I'm still on my knees, with tears gently streaming down my face. You are unsure what to do. 'I just wanted to fit in,' I say quietly. 'I just thought if I rebranded as a nature-loving local lad, the world would love me again.' You put your arms under my armpits and heave me up out of the ditch I appear to have fallen into. You're definitely stronger than at the start of the book.

'This has all been great and everything,' you say as you help me sit on a stone wall, 'but it's getting late – it's probably about time I started heading back.' I slump over. 'Yeah, that makes sense, I should probably head back too. Mairead gets annoyed when I stay out too late, and I still have to give her son his evening German lesson. We're doing tools vocabulary – I've been trying to teach him how to pronounce the word for screwdriver for days now.' 'What is it?' you ask. '*Kreuzschlitzschraubenzieher*,' I say, some spittle flying out of my mouth as I do. 'What a beautiful language,' you say, wiping your face. We stand there awkwardly, unsure of how to say goodbye to each other.

'Anyway, as I said,' – you gesture up the road – 'I'd better be going, and I'm sure Mairead is worried . . .' 'Yes yes,' I interrupt, 'you get going back to the city, I don't envy you at all, all the noise and the chaos. No thank you! I won't be going back there anytime soon.' 'Ha, exactly. Anyway, bye now, thanks for everything,' you say, and you start walking off, before pausing and turning back towards me, still slumped miserably on the stone wall.

'You know, I'm just putting this out there, but we have a spare room in our flat at the minute. If you were interested.' My head jolts up. 'Are you serious?' I try to keep the joy out of my voice. 'What's the rent?' I hop off the wall. You start backtracking. 'I mean, it's not much of a "room" really, more of a long cupboard with space for a mattress. It doesn't have windows. I don't think we could charge you rent for it . . .' 'I'll take it,' I interrupt again before you can change your mind, 'and I can move in right now.' 'But what about the countryside?' you ask, incredulous. 'What happened to being at one with nature and the city being a waste of time, the future is Mother Nature and all that?' I don't hear your words; my eyes are looking at the sky, filled with a glowing hope. 'Public transport,' I whisper softly to the clouds, 'properly made oat-milk lattes.' I walk towards you and grab your arm.

'We need to get out of here quickly or we'll have a very angry Irish woman on our tail, demanding we teach her son the nominative case.'

I pull you down the road, looking over my shoulder as I do. Confused by the sudden change of events, you allow yourself to be dragged along. 'I'm a very quiet roommate, you'll barely notice me,' I prattle excitedly as we walk. 'I do a Mongolian throat-singing exercise at 5 a.m. to start the day, but I've been told it's a very soothing sound. Can I book the common living area Mondays, Tuesdays and Friday evenings? My slam poetry group is looking for a new meet-up spot. This is going to be *so* much fun.' You stutter a response to my barrage of chatter. 'Maybe we'll have to talk to the other roommates, maybe this isn't a good idea . . .' You sound panicked. 'I thought you loved the countryside? Don't you want to stay here?' you plead. I ruffle your hair. 'Oh my sweet naive friend, you're so behind the times, the countryside influencer thing, that's so done. I'm over it and so is everyone else. You know what people are interested in? Bitcoin and Forex trading. That's how you make the big bucks. Say, you couldn't lend me some hard cash? Just to get me on my feet. We can hash out the details later.'

My face is bright with energy, you can almost hear my brain humming. Are those the opening chords of Thin Lizzy's 'The Boys Are Back In Town', playing from a speaker somewhere in the distance? 'Guess who just got back today,' I sing, as you look at me, slightly terrified, 'them wild-eyed boys that had been away . . .'